The Dancing Heart:
Na'ima's Journey of Kindness and Dreams

A Story of Kindness, Perseverance, and Achieving Your Goals

Written by: Alisa L. Grace

Illustrated By: naqsa-art

Dedication:

To Na'ima, may your passion for dance always light your way, and may your kind heart and leadership inspire others to shine brightly, too.

This story may encourage readers to embrace your dreams, celebrate your unique talents, and always strive for kindness and excellence.

A Letter to Na'ima:

Dear Na'ima,

This book celebrates you – your vibrant spirit, love for dance, and kind heart that shines so brightly. As you twirl and leap through these pages, remember that your dedication and passion will take you far on your incredible journey.

Embrace every opportunity to learn and grow on the dance floor and the world around you. Whether mastering a challenging new step or helping a friend, your determination and positive attitude will guide you toward your dreams.

Never be afraid to express yourself through dance. Let your movements speak volumes, telling stories of joy, resilience, and the beautiful rhythm that beats within your heart.

Remember that your kindness is a gift. It has the power to uplift others, create lasting friendships, and make the world a more beautiful place. Always lead with your heart, Na'ima, and inspire those around you with your incredible energy.

Believe in yourself, just as we believe in you. You have the strength, talent, and kind spirit to achieve your dreams and positively impact the world. So go out there, dance your heart out, and let your light shine!

With love and encouragement,

Your NeNe!

A Letter to Parents

Dear Parents,

As you embark on this exciting journey with Na'ima and her dancing dreams, we invite you to personalize the experience and make it even more meaningful for your child.

Throughout the story, you'll find sections titled "Ways to Support Na'ima" and "Tips for Parents." While the name "Na'ima" is used in these sections, it represents your child.

Imagine replacing "Na'ima" with your own child's name as you read these sections. This simple act can create a deeper connection and make the advice and encouragement feel more personal and relevant to your family.

We believe that every child has a unique dance within them, a passion waiting to be discovered and nurtured. This book is designed to inspire young dancers, dreamers, and anyone who loves a good story about friendship, family, and the power of believing in yourself.

We hope that "The Dancing Heart" will not only entertain your child but also empower them to embrace their dreams, develop essential life skills, and discover the incredible strength and kindness within their own hearts.

Happy reading!

With warm wishes,

The Author

Contents

Introduction: 7

Chapter 1: The Big Announcement 10

Chapter 2: Planning for Success 16

Chapter 3: Time Flies When You're Dancing ... 21

Chapter 4: Remembering the Steps 26

Chapter 5: Staying Focused and Flexible 30

Chapter 6: Facing Challenges with Grace 35

Chapter 7: The Power of Teamwork 40

Chapter 8: Opening Night Jitters 45

Chapter 9: Shining Bright 49

Chapter 10: A Dream Come True 54

Introduction:

Na'ima, a vibrant 10-year-old with a heart full of rhythm and a passion for dance, is about to embark on an exciting journey. With her sights set on a grand performance at the Dr. Phillips Center in Orlando, she's determined to give it her all. Alongside her beloved 8-year-old sister, Naudia, Na'ima navigates the challenges and joys of rehearsals, schoolwork, and family life.

But Na'ima is more than just a talented dancer. She's a natural leader with a kind heart and a desire to help others. This story follows her as she learns valuable life lessons about perseverance, teamwork, and the importance of a positive attitude. Join Na'ima as she twirls, leaps, and grows, discovering the incredible power within herself to achieve her dreams and inspire those around her.

Chapter 1: The Big Announcement

Chapter 1:
The Big Announcement

The aroma of pancakes filled the air as Na'ima bounced into the kitchen, her braids swinging with every excited step. "Morning, Mom! Guess what?" she exclaimed, her eyes sparkling.

"What is it, my little dancing queen?" her mom asked, flipping a golden pancake onto a plate.

"Miss Anya announced that our dance recital will be at the Dr. Phillips Center this year!" Na'ima squealed, barely able to contain her excitement. "Can you imagine? We'll be performing on a real stage!"

Her mom smiled. "That's wonderful news, Na'ima! I know how much you and Naudia have looked forward to this."

Na'ima's younger sister, Naudia, entered the kitchen, her sleepy eyes widening at the news. "The Dr. Phillips Center? Wow!"

Their 5-year-old brother, Nyrie, piped up, "Can I come to watch?"

"Of course, sweetie," their dad said, ruffling Nyrie's hair. "We'll all be there to cheer you on."

As Na'ima savored her breakfast, her mind raced with possibilities. This year's recital was going to be amazing. She could already picture herself gliding across the stage, the lights shining down, the audience captivated by her every move. She knew it would take dedication and hard work, but Na'ima was ready for the challenge.

10-Minute Activity

My Dance Journey Visualization & Goal Setting

Directions:

1. Find a quiet and comfortable space where you can relax.

2. Close your eyes and imagine yourself on stage at the Dr. Phillips Center. Visualize the lights, the audience, and how it feels to perform.

3. Now, think about your dance goals. What do you want to achieve as a dancer? What skills do you want to improve?

4. Open your eyes and write down your dance goals in a notebook or journal. Be specific and realistic.

   _____
   _____
   _____

5. Decorate your goal page with drawings or images that inspire you.

Materials: Notebook or journal, pens/pencils, optional: colored pencils, magazines for cut-outs.

Transformative Aspect: This activity encourages self-reflection, visualization, and goal setting, key skills for success in any area of life.

Chapter 2: Planning for Success

Chapter 2: Planning for Success

Na'ima stared at the long list of dance steps Miss Anya had given them for their new routine. It seemed overwhelming! "How am I ever going to learn all this?" she wondered.

Her mom, noticing her worried expression, sat down beside her. "It seems like a lot right now, but remember what we discussed? Breaking big tasks into smaller ones makes them much easier to handle."

Together, they divided the dance routine into smaller sections. Na'ima decided to focus on learning the first four steps perfectly before moving on to the next. She also started using a planner to keep track of her rehearsal schedule and other commitments.

Later that week, the family headed to Disney World. Na'ima, armed with her planner and a map, helped her parents organize their day. "First, we'll ride Space Mountain," she declared, "then we'll have lunch at Cosmic Ray's Starlight Cafe, and then we'll head to Fantasyland!"

By planning ahead and breaking down their day into manageable chunks, they could experience all their favorite rides and shows without feeling rushed or overwhelmed.

10-Minute Activity

"Dance Routine Breakdown"

Directions:

1. Take a complex dance routine or a challenging piece of choreography.

2. Divide the routine into smaller sections (e.g., intro, verse, chorus, and bridge) on a large sheet of paper.

3. For each section, write down the key steps or movements. Use abbreviations or symbols if needed.

_____
_____
_____

4. If it's helpful, draw simple stick figures to illustrate the steps.

5. Practice each section separately before putting them all together.

Materials: Large sheet of paper, pens/pencils, optional: colored markers.

Transformative Aspect: This activity teaches the crucial skill of breaking down large tasks into smaller, more manageable parts, promoting organization and reducing overwhelm.

Chapter 3: Time Flies When You're Dancing

Chapter 3:
Time Flies When You're Dancing

Na'ima loved spending time at the playground with Naudia and Nyrie. But with dance rehearsals, schoolwork, and family time, it was sometimes hard to fit everything in.

"Na'ima, can you push me on the swings?" Nyrie pleaded.

"Just a minute, Nyrie," she replied. "I need to finish my math homework first."

Na'ima was learning to estimate how long different activities would take. She realized that if she focused on her homework now, she would have plenty of time to play with her siblings afterward.

She also started creating a weekly schedule, allocating specific times for homework, dance practice, playtime, and even some quiet time for herself. This helped her prioritize her activities and make sure she had enough time for everything she wanted to do.

10-Minute Activity:

My Daily Schedule

Directions:

1. Take a blank sheet of paper and divide it into sections representing different times of the day (e.g., morning, afternoon, evening).

2. Write down your typical activities for each time slot, including school, dance rehearsals, meals, homework, and free time.

   _____
   _____
   _____

3. Use different colors to represent different types of activities.

4. Reflect on your schedule: Are there any areas where you feel rushed or overwhelmed? Are there any activities you'd like to make more time for?

   _____
   _____
   _____

5. Adjust your schedule to create a better balance and improve your time management.

Materials: Blank sheet of paper, pens/pencils, colored markers.

Transformative Aspect: This activity promotes self-awareness and time management skills, helping children learn to prioritize activities and create a balanced schedule.

Chapter 4: Remembering the Steps

Chapter 4:
Remembering the Steps

Learning a new dance routine involved remembering a complex sequence of steps. Na'ima sometimes struggled to keep them all in order.

Miss Anya suggested using visual aids. "Try drawing simple pictures or diagrams to represent each step," she advised.

Na'ima found this incredibly helpful. She created a visual chart with stick figures demonstrating the different moves. She also started playing memory games with her siblings, which helped improve her ability to recall information.

When Nyrie had trouble memorizing his spelling words, Na'ima used her new skills to help him. She created flashcards with colorful pictures and made a silly song to help him remember the spellings.

10-Minute Activity

Memory Palace for Dance Moves

Directions:

1. Think of a familiar place, like your home or your school.

2. Imagine walking through this place and assigning each dance step in your routine to a specific location or object. For example, the first step might be associated with the front door, the second step with the hallway, etc.

3. Create a mental picture of each step happening in that location.

4. To recall the routine, mentally walk through your "memory palace" and retrieve the steps from their assigned locations.

Materials: None (this is a mental exercise).

Transformative Aspect: This activity introduces the memory palace technique, a powerful memory strategy that can be applied to various learning situations.

Chapter 5: Staying Focused and Flexible

Chapter 5:
Staying Focused and Flexible

During one rehearsal, Miss Anya announced a change in the dance routine. "We're going to add a new sequence in the middle," she said.

Na'ima felt a surge of frustration. She had already learned the original routine so well! But she took a deep breath, reminding herself to stay flexible.

She listened carefully to Miss Anya's instructions and focused on learning the new steps. She also realized that this change offered an opportunity to make the dance even more exciting.

Na'ima was learning to manage her emotions and adapt to unexpected situations. She understood that things don't always go as planned, and that's okay.

10-Minute Activity

The Unexpected Change Challenge

Directions:

1. Choose a familiar activity, like building a LEGO structure or drawing a picture.

2. Start the activity as planned.

3. Midway through, introduce an unexpected change. For example, swap out some bricks for different shapes or colors if building with LEGOs. If drawing, switch to a different drawing tool or change the subject.

4. Notice your initial reaction to the change. Do you feel frustrated or resistant?

_____
_____
_____

5. Take a deep breath and try to embrace the change. How can you adapt your plan or approach? Can you find a creative solution?

_____
_____
_____

Materials: Varies depending on the chosen activity (e.g., LEGO bricks, drawing supplies).

Transformative Aspect: This activity helps children develop flexibility and adaptability, teaching them to cope with unexpected situations and find creative solutions.

Chapter 6: Facing Challenges with Grace

Chapter 6:
Facing Challenges with Grace

Na'ima loved the feeling of soaring through the air, her body weightless as she leaped and twirled. But one move kept tripping her up—the fouetté turn. It required a quick, precise whipping motion of the leg, and Na'ima couldn't seem to get it right.

She practiced tirelessly, but the more she tried, the more frustrated she became. "I'll never get this," she sighed, sinking onto the dance studio floor.

Miss Anya, noticing her discouragement, knelt beside her. "Na'ima, remember that every dancer faces challenges. The key is to approach them with grace and perseverance."

She showed Na'ima some techniques to improve her balance and control. "Don't focus on the difficulty," Miss Anya encouraged. "Focus on the feeling of the movement, the flow of your body."

Na'ima took a deep breath and tried again, focusing on the fluidity of the turn rather than the fear of falling. Slowly but surely, she started to get the hang of it. With each successful turn, her confidence grew.

10-Minute Activity

My 'I Can Do It!' Mantra

Directions:

1. Think about a challenge in dance or any other area of your life.

2. Create a short, positive phrase or mantra you can repeat to yourself when you feel discouraged. For example, "I can do it!", "I'm strong and capable," or "I'll keep trying until I succeed."

3. Write your mantra on paper and decorate it with inspiring images or symbols.

_____
_____
_____

4. Practice saying your mantra out loud with confidence and conviction.

5. Whenever you face a challenge, remember your mantra and repeat it to yourself to boost your self-belief and motivation.

Materials: Paper, pens/pencils, optional: colored markers, magazines for cut-outs.

Transformative Aspect: This activity helps children develop a positive self-image and cultivate a growth mindset, encouraging them to embrace challenges and believe in their ability to overcome obstacles.

Chapter 6: Facing Challenges with Grace

Chapter 7:
The Power of Teamwork

Miss Anya had a surprise for the class. "We're going to be learning a new routine," she announced, "and it's a group dance!"

Na'ima was excited. She loved dancing with her friends and knew that working together would bring a new dimension to their performance.

The routine was challenging, requiring them to synchronize their movements and support each other. At first, they bumped into each other and struggled to keep up. But with practice and encouragement, they started to move as one.

With her natural leadership skills, Na'ima helped her teammates stay focused and motivated. "We can do this!" she'd say, offering a helping hand or a word of encouragement.

10-Minute Activity

Teamwork Challenge

Directions:

1. Gather a group of friends or family members.

2. Choose a collaborative task that requires teamwork, such as building a tower with blocks, creating a group drawing, or solving a puzzle together.

3. Assign roles or responsibilities to each team member.

4. Work together to complete the task, communicating effectively and supporting each other.

5. After completing the task, reflect on the experience. How did teamwork contribute to your success? What challenges did you face, and how did you overcome them?

_____
_____
_____

Materials: Varies depending on the chosen activity (e.g., blocks, drawing supplies, puzzles).

Transformative Aspect: This activity promotes collaboration, communication, and problem-solving skills, highlighting the importance of teamwork and collective effort in achieving a shared goal.

Chapter 8: Opening Night Jitters

Chapter 8: Opening Night Jitters

The day of the recital finally arrived. Na'ima was excited but also a little nervous. This was the most significant stage she had ever performed on, and she wanted to do her best.

Backstage, the energy was buzzing. Dancers were stretching, adjusting their costumes, and practicing their steps. Na'ima could hear the murmur of the audience beyond the curtain.

Suddenly, a wave of nervousness washed over her. Her palms started to sweat, and her heart pounded in her chest. "What if I forget the steps?" she worried. "What if I trip and fall?"

Her mom, sensing her anxiety, gave her a reassuring hug. "Na'ima, you've worked so hard for this. Just remember to breathe and have fun. We're all here to support you."

Na'ima took a deep breath and closed her eyes, visualizing herself on stage, dancing confidently and gracefully. She reminded herself of all the hours of practice, the challenges she had overcome, and the joy that dance brought her.

10-Minute Activity:

Calming Breath and Visualization

Directions:

1. Find a quiet and comfortable space where you can relax.

2. Close your eyes and take slow, deep breaths. Inhale through your nose, fill your belly with air, and exhale slowly through your mouth.

3. As you breathe, imagine yourself performing confidently and gracefully on stage. Visualize the audience applauding and cheering.

4. Continue breathing deeply and visualizing your success for several minutes.

5. When you feel calmer and more focused, open your eyes.

Materials: None (this is a relaxation exercise).

Transformative Aspect: This activity introduces mindfulness techniques, such as deep breathing and visualization, to help children manage anxiety and promote a sense of calm and focus.

Chapter 9: Shining Bright

Chapter 9:
Shining Bright

The lights dimmed, the music swelled, and the curtain rose. Na'ima took her place on stage, her heart filled with excitement and determination.

As the music began, all her nervousness melted away. She moved with grace and precision, her body expressing the rhythm and emotion of the dance. She felt the energy of the audience, their applause washing over her like a wave.

At that moment, Na'ima was utterly in her element. She was a dancer, sharing her passion with the world. She flowed through the routines, her movements fluid and expressive.

10-Minute Activity

My Performance Reflection

Directions:

1. After a performance or presentation, take some time to reflect on your experience.

2. Write down your thoughts and feelings about the performance in a journal or notebook. What went well? What could you improve?

   _____
   _____
   _____

3. Focus on the positive aspects of your performance and acknowledge your accomplishments.

4. Identify areas for growth and set goals for future performances.

Materials: Journal or notebook, pens/pencils.

Transformative Aspect: This activity encourages self-reflection and self-assessment, helping children learn from their experiences and set goals for continuous improvement.

Chapter 10: A Dream Come True

Chapter 10:
A Dream Come True

The final notes of the music faded away, and the applause erupted. Na'ima and her fellow dancers took a bow, their hearts filled with pride and joy.

Na'ima felt a sense of accomplishment wash over her as the curtain closed. She had faced challenges, overcome her nerves, and performed well. She had danced her heart out on the stage of the Dr. Phillips Center, and her dream had come true.

But more importantly, she had learned valuable lessons about perseverance, teamwork, and the power of a positive attitude. She had discovered that she could achieve anything she set her mind to with dedication and kindness.

Backstage, her family showered her with hugs and congratulations. "You were amazing, Na'ima!" her mom exclaimed, her eyes sparkling with pride.

"We're so proud of you," her dad added, beaming.

Na'ima grinned, her heart overflowing with happiness. She knew this was just the beginning of her dance journey, and she couldn't wait to see what the future held.

10-Minute Activity

Gratitude Journal

- **Directions:**

    1. Take a few minutes each day to write down things you are grateful for.

    2. These could be big things, like your family and friends, or small things, like a sunny day or a delicious meal.

    3. Reflect on how these things make you feel and why you appreciate them.

- **Materials:** Journal or notebook, pens/pencils.

- **Transformative Aspect:** This activity fosters gratitude and positive thinking, helping children appreciate the good things in their lives and develop a sense of optimism and well-being.

Ways to Support Na'ima:
(Na'ima represents your young dancer)

Positive Reinforcement: Praise her efforts and dedication, focusing on the process rather than just the outcome. For example, instead of saying, "You were amazing!" after a performance, try saying, "I loved how expressive you were on stage, and I could see how much hard work you put into learning those steps." This helps Na'ima understand that your appreciation goes beyond the final product and recognizes her commitment to growth.

Provide Resources: Ensure she has comfortable dancewear, shoes for each dance style, and a dedicated practice space where she can focus without distractions. This might involve setting up a corner of her room with a mirror and a barre or finding a quiet space where she can spread out and move freely.

Attend Performances: Show your support by attending her rehearsals and performances. Your presence lets her know that you value her passion and are invested in her journey as a dancer. Even if you can't make it to every event, try to prioritize the ones that are most important to her.

Active Listening: Listen to Na'ima's thoughts and feelings about her dance experiences. Ask open-ended questions like "What did you enjoy most about rehearsal today?" or "What are you most excited about for the recital?" This shows her that you care about her perspective and are interested in her development as a dancer and a person.

Facilitate Goal Setting: Help Na'ima set realistic and achievable goals for her dance journey. These goals involve mastering a specific technique, learning a new dance style, or increasing her flexibility or stamina. Breaking down larger goals into smaller milestones can make them feel less daunting and provide a sense of accomplishment.

Encourage Exploration: While Na'ima may have her favorite dance styles, encourage her to explore different forms and techniques. This could involve attending workshops, trying out new classes, or watching performances of diverse dance styles. Exposure to various dance forms can broaden her horizons, spark new interests, and deepen her appreciation for the art of movement.

Additional Interactive Resource List:

Organizational Tools:

Google Calendar: A free online calendar that allows Na'ima to schedule events, set reminders, and share her calendar with family members. This can help her visualize her commitments and manage her time effectively.

Trello: A visual project management tool that uses boards, lists, and cards to organize tasks and track progress. Na'ima can create boards for different areas of her life (dance, school, chores) and break down larger tasks into smaller, manageable steps.

Todoist: A task management app that allows Na'ima to create to-do lists, set deadlines, and prioritize tasks. It offers features like recurring tasks, sub-tasks, and collaboration options, making it a versatile tool for staying organized.

Time Management Resources:

Time Timer: A visual timer that displays the passage of time with a red disk that gradually disappears. This can help Na'ima develop a sense of time and stay focused on tasks.

Toggl Track: A time-tracking app that allows Na'ima to track how much time she spends on different activities. This can help her identify time management challenges and adjust her schedule.

Focus Keeper: An app that uses the Pomodoro Technique, breaking work sessions into 25-minute intervals with short breaks in between. This can help Na'ima improve her focus and productivity.

Working Memory Games:

Lumosity: A brain training app with games designed to improve memory, attention, and other cognitive skills.

Elevate Another brain training app with games focusing on reading, writing, speaking, and math skills.

Cogmed Working Memory Training: A comprehensive program to improve working memory capacity. It involves a series of challenging exercises that adapt to the user's performance.

Mindfulness and Self-Control Apps:

Headspace: A meditation app with guided meditations for all ages, including sessions specifically designed for children.

Calm: Another popular meditation app with calming exercises, sleep stories, and nature sounds.

GoNoodle: A website and app with movement breaks, mindfulness activities, and videos that promote physical and emotional well-being.

Educational Websites and Apps:

Khan Academy: A free online learning platform with lessons and exercises in various subjects, including math, science, and humanities.

Quizlet: A learning tool that allows Na'ima to create flashcards, play learning games, and test her knowledge.

BrainPop: An educational website with animated videos and interactive quizzes on various topics.

Additional Resources:

Books:

"Tallulah's Tutu" by Marilyn Singer: This delightful story follows Tallulah, a young girl who is initially hesitant about ballet class but soon discovers the joy of movement and the magic of expressing herself through dance. This book can help Na'ima relate to the challenges and triumphs of a budding dancer and foster a love for the art form.

"Firebird" by Misty Copeland: This beautifully illustrated book, inspired by the iconic ballet, tells the story of a young girl who overcomes self-doubt and embraces her unique talent to become a graceful and powerful dancer. Misty Copeland, a renowned ballerina, is a role model for aspiring dancers, demonstrating that dreams can become reality with dedication and perseverance.

"Dancing in the Wings" by Debbie Allen: This empowering story celebrates individuality and self-acceptance. It follows a young girl with long legs who learns to embrace her unique physicality and find her place in the world of dance. This book can inspire Na'ima to celebrate her own strengths and express herself authentically.

"Bunheads" by Sophie Flack: This engaging novel follows Hannah, a young dancer who navigates the challenges and excitement of attending a prestigious ballet school. This book offers a realistic portrayal of the dedication and discipline required to pursue a career in dance, while also highlighting the importance of friendship and perseverance.

Amazon Kids+ Books:

"The Ballet Book" by Darcey Bussell: This interactive book introduces young readers to the world of ballet with engaging illustrations, fun facts, and simple instructions for basic ballet steps.

"Hip Hop Dance" by Katie Marsico: This book explores the history and culture of hip-hop dance with vibrant photographs and step-by-step guides to popular moves.

"Lola, the Dancing Dog" by Anna McQuinn: This heartwarming story follows Lola, a dog who loves to dance and brings joy to everyone around her. This book celebrates the power of dance to connect people and express emotions.

"The Dance Class" by Deanna Caswell and Janet Wilson: This charming book follows a group of young dancers as they learn new steps, prepare for a recital, and develop a love for dance.

"Ellie, Engineer: The Dancing Machine" by Jackson Pearce: This book combines STEM and dance, as Ellie uses her engineering skills to create a dancing robot for a competition. This can inspire Na'ima to explore the connections between different disciplines and think creatively about problem-solving.

Videos:

Ballet:

- "Angelina Ballerina" series (Available on Amazon Prime Video): This animated series follows the adventures of Angelina, a charming mouse who dreams of becoming a ballerina. The show introduces young viewers to ballet, with engaging stories and delightful dance sequences.

- "The Nutcracker" animated movie (Available on Amazon Prime Video): This classic tale, brought to life through animation, tells the story of Clara and her magical journey with the Nutcracker Prince. The film features beautiful ballet sequences set to Tchaikovsky's iconic score, introducing children to the beauty and wonder of this beloved ballet.

- Search for "Royal Ballet School" or "beginner ballet for kids" on YouTube for instructional videos. These videos offer step-by-step guidance for learning basic ballet techniques, from pliés and tendus to jumps and turns.

Hip Hop:

- "Kidz Bop Dance Along" videos (Available on Amazon Prime Video): These high-energy videos feature kids performing popular dance moves to kid-friendly versions of popular songs. They offer a fun and engaging way for Na'ima to learn hip-hop choreography and express herself through movement.

- Search for "hip hop dance for kids beginners" or "easy hip hop dance tutorials" on YouTube: These tutorials break down hip-hop moves into manageable steps, making it easy for Na'ima to learn the basics and build her confidence.

General Dance Videos:

- "Just Dance Kids" videos (Available on Amazon Prime Video): This interactive video game series encourages kids to get up and move, with fun choreography set to popular songs. It's an excellent way for Na'ima to practice her dance skills, improve her coordination, and have fun with friends and family. * Search for "children's dance videos" or "dance along songs for kids" on YouTube: These videos offer various dance styles and choreography, from contemporary and jazz to folk and cultural dances. They can inspire Na'ima to explore different forms of movement and discover new ways to express herself.

Tips for Parents:

Encourage a Growth Mindset: Help Na'ima understand that mistakes are part of learning and that effort and perseverance lead to improvement. Focus on praising her effort, persistence, and progress rather than just her natural talent. This will help her develop a love of learning and resilience that will serve her well in all areas of life.

Foster a Love of Movement: Encourage various physical activities, not just dance, to promote overall fitness and well-being. This could involve playing sports, swimming, biking, hiking, or engaging in active play outdoors. A variety of physical activities helps Na'ima develop different muscle groups, improve her coordination, and maintain a healthy lifestyle.

Balance is Key: Help Na'ima balance her passion for dance with other important aspects of her life, such as school, family time, and rest. Ensure she has enough time for homework, social activities, and relaxation. A balanced lifestyle contributes to her overall well-being and prevents burnout.

Nurture Creativity: Encourage Na'ima to explore her creativity beyond dance, whether through drawing, writing, music, or other forms of self-expression. This helps her develop a well-rounded personality and discover new talents and passions.

Support Healthy Habits: Promote healthy eating habits and ensure Na'ima gets enough sleep. Proper nutrition and adequate rest are essential for her physical and mental well-being, especially as she engages in demanding dance training.

Open Communication: Maintain open communication with Na'ima about her dance experiences, feelings, and any challenges she may face. Create a safe space to express herself and seek support when needed.

Celebrate the Journey: Remember to celebrate Na'ima's achievements and milestones along the way. Acknowledge her hard work, dedication, and progress, no matter how big or small. This helps her build confidence, stay motivated, and develop a lifelong love of dance.

Na'ima loves to dance! Ballet, hip-hop, jazz – she loves it all. And this year's recital is extra special: it's at the Dr. Phillips Center in Orlando!

But with rehearsals, schoolwork, and family life, Na'ima has a lot to juggle. Luckily, she's a natural leader with a kind heart and a passion for helping others. Join Na'ima as she learns to:

Break down big tasks into smaller steps
Manage her time effectively
Boost her memory with fun techniques
Stay focused and flexible even when things change
Overcome challenges with grace and a positive attitude

Filled with exciting dance adventures, family fun at Disney World, and heartwarming moments with her siblings, "The Dancing Heart" is a story about the power of perseverance, the importance of kindness, and the joy of achieving your dreams.

This book includes fun 10-minute activities in every chapter to help young readers develop essential life skills!

www.ingramcontent.com/pod-product-compliance
Lightning Source LLC
Chambersburg PA
CBHW050456110426
42743CB00017B/3385